STEPHEN BIESTY

GREECE

in spectacular cross-section

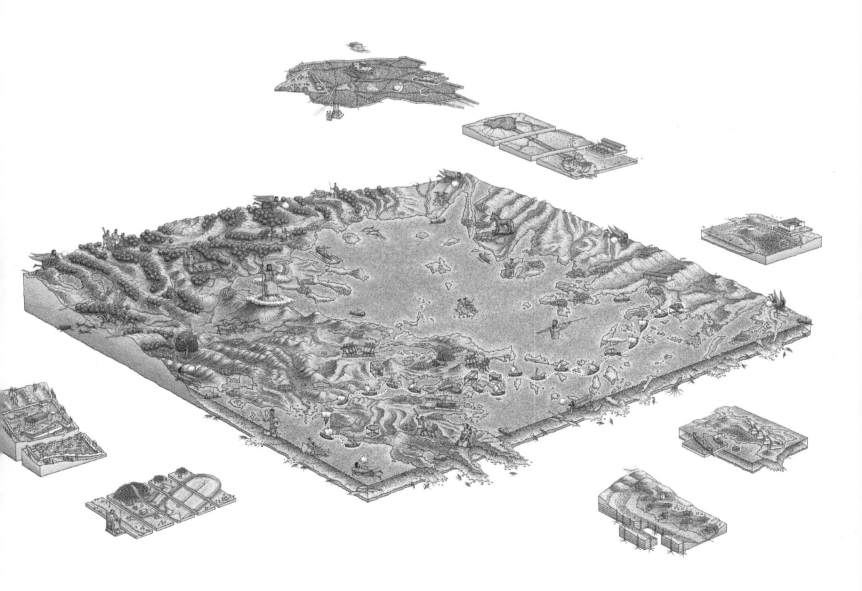

Text by Stewart Ross

Consultant: James Morwood

OXFORD

UNIVERSITY PRESS

'Why I am proud to be a Greek'
by Neleus, son of Aristagoras the Milesian

Aristagoras   *paidagogos*

    Mother   Helen   Peri

          Penelope   Neleus

I am proud to be a Greek because we are the world's most civilized and powerful people. Three things show this.

First, we dwell with the gods: on Mount Olympus in the Greek state of Thessaly live Zeus, king of the gods, and eleven other mighty deities. Such neighbours are the greatest honour, but they are easily angered and we have to take care not to annoy them. Everything that goes wrong is a punishment from the gods for our folly.

Second, our way of life is the best. We are organized into prosperous, well-run states, each with its own capital city and surrounding countryside. Athens, the richest and grandest city-state, has overseas settlements and allies like Miletus, where we live. Sparta, Athens' rival, is a famous military power. All Greeks share the same wonderful language, with its rich traditions of poetry, philosophy and history. We are great thinkers: who else knows as much about government, science and astronomy? We use silver money, too, and hold fantastic athletic games.

Third, we proved our greatness when we defeated the invading Persians. The first Greek triumph was when the Athenians and Plataeans smashed the enemy at Marathon. The Spartans led by Leonidas then brilliantly held up their advance at Thermopylae. Finally, the Athenian fleet won a great victory at Salamis and the Persian army was overwhelmed at Plataea. The fighting ended about thirty years ago.

The only thing that might damage our wonderful civilization is if we fight amongst ourselves. This did happen a while back, when Athens and Sparta fell out. Today we are still enjoying the fruits of the thirty-year truce they made just after I was born.

Contents

Peri

Greece

Neleus

Our journey

I'm Neleus, aged almost 12, and I've just returned from the fantastic journey shown on this map. My father, the grain merchant Aristagoras, took me and my younger brother Periander ('Peri', who is 10) to Athens. Dad had important business to sort out there. We then sailed to Delphi, where we consulted the world-famous oracle. Finally, the gods decided our family's future in a wrestling match at the Olympic Games. Cool trip, eh?

DAY 32

The theatre of Dionysus
This famous theatre nestles beneath the city's Acropolis, on which stands the mighty Parthenon, the temple of Athene.

DAY 29

The Agora at Athens
The open space at the heart of the city, surrounded by important public buildings, commonly serves as a market place.

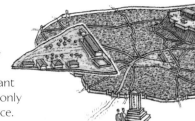

Artemis
The virgin deity Artemis was the goddess of hunting, animals and childbirth. Her temple at Ephesus was one of the Seven Wonders of the ancient world.

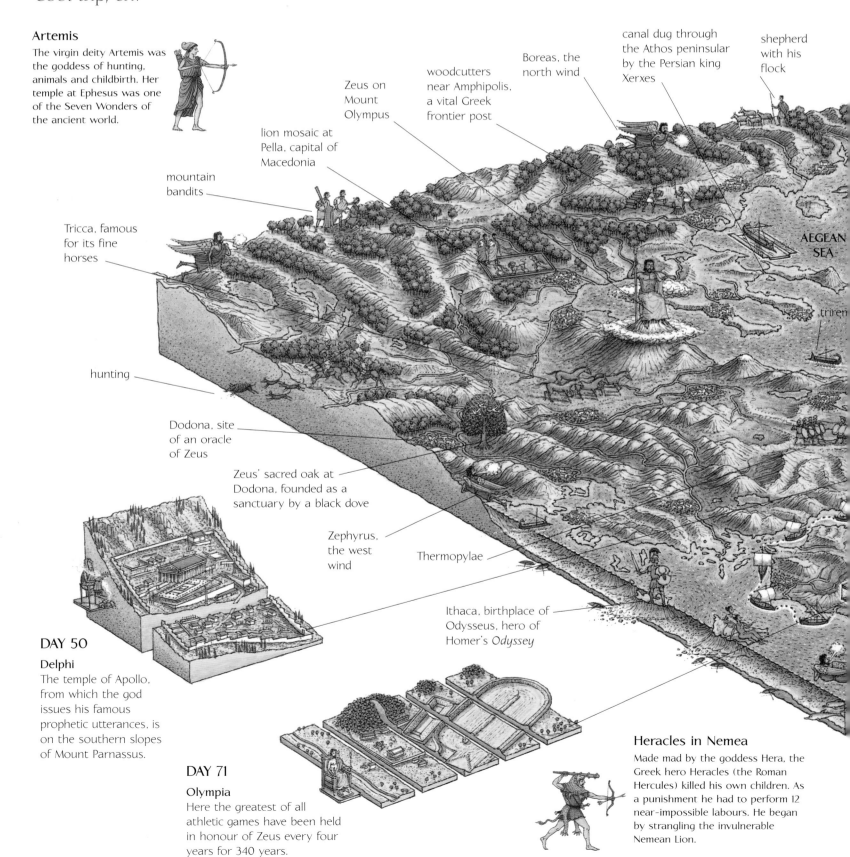

mountain bandits

lion mosaic at Pella, capital of Macedonia

Zeus on Mount Olympus

woodcutters near Amphipolis, a vital Greek frontier post

Boreas, the north wind

canal dug through the Athos peninsular by the Persian king Xerxes

shepherd with his flock

Tricca, famous for its fine horses

AEGEAN SEA

trireme

hunting

Dodona, site of an oracle of Zeus

Zeus' sacred oak at Dodona, founded as a sanctuary by a black dove

Zephyrus, the west wind

Thermopylae

Ithaca, birthplace of Odysseus, hero of Homer's *Odyssey*

DAY 50

Delphi
The temple of Apollo, from which the god issues his famous prophetic utterances, is on the southern slopes of Mount Parnassus.

DAY 71

Olympia
Here the greatest of all athletic games have been held in honour of Zeus every four years for 340 years.

Heracles in Nemea
Made mad by the goddess Hera, the Greek hero Heracles (the Roman Hercules) killed his own children. As a punishment he had to perform 12 near-impossible labours. He began by strangling the invulnerable Nemean Lion.

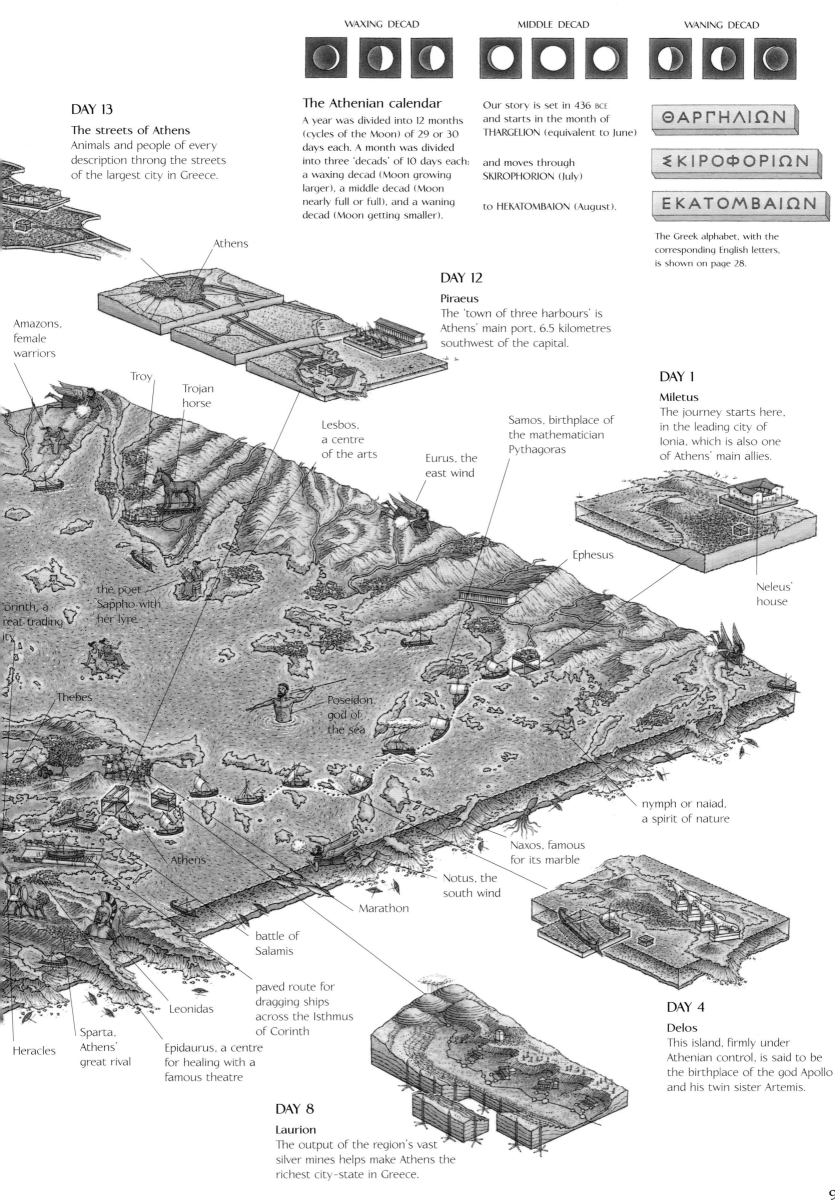

DAY 13

The streets of Athens
Animals and people of every description throng the streets of the largest city in Greece.

The Athenian calendar

A year was divided into 12 months (cycles of the Moon) of 29 or 30 days each. A month was divided into three 'decads' of 10 days each: a waxing decad (Moon growing larger), a middle decad (Moon nearly full or full), and a waning decad (Moon getting smaller).

Our story is set in 436 BCE and starts in the month of THARGELION (equivalent to June)

and moves through SKIROPHORION (July)

to HEKATOMBAION (August).

ΘΑΡΓΗΛΙΩΝ

ΣΚΙΡΟΦΟΡΙΩΝ

ΕΚΑΤΟΜΒΑΙΩΝ

The Greek alphabet, with the corresponding English letters, is shown on page 28.

Athens

Amazons, female warriors

DAY 12

Piraeus
The 'town of three harbours' is Athens' main port, 6.5 kilometres southwest of the capital.

DAY 1

Miletus
The journey starts here, in the leading city of Ionia, which is also one of Athens' main allies.

Troy

Trojan horse

Lesbos, a centre of the arts

Samos, birthplace of the mathematician Pythagoras

Eurus, the east wind

Ephesus

Neleus' house

Corinth, a great trading city

the poet Sappho with her lyre

Thebes

Poseidon, god of the sea

nymph or naiad, a spirit of nature

Naxos, famous for its marble

Athens

Notus, the south wind

Marathon

battle of Salamis

paved route for dragging ships across the Isthmus of Corinth

Leonidas

Sparta, Athens' great rival

Epidaurus, a centre for healing with a famous theatre

Heracles

DAY 8

Laurion
The output of the region's vast silver mines helps make Athens the richest city-state in Greece.

DAY 4

Delos
This island, firmly under Athenian control, is said to be the birthplace of the god Apollo and his twin sister Artemis.

9

At home in Miletus

We didn't sleep much the night before we left. Dad had a noisy farewell party – he was in a good mood because he'd just heard from Aspasia. She's the Milesian girlfriend of Pericles, a really important Athenian politician. Her letter said Pericles would help dad in the Athenian courts. After packing, Peri and I argued for hours about the Milesian wrestler Thrasyboulos. Peri reckoned 'Boulos' was certain to win the Olympics. I wasn't so sure.

women
City life for respectable Greek women was very limited. They had few rights and were expected to spend most of their time doing tedious work indoors. Women living in the countryside were far less restricted.

terracotta roof tiles

lamp-lighter slave

Neleus

Peri

sick child with pet ducks

cheese

onions

dried fruit

herbs

household altar

mud brick

provisions for the voyage

bread-making

pet quails

evening tuition

slave washing a guest's feet

healthy diet
Home-made bread, fresh fish and meat, vegetables and fruit – the diet in Neleus' household is very healthy. It is less so for poorer people, who rely heavily on bread at every meal.

symposium
Guests arrive late for Aristagoras' farewell symposium – an all-male drinking party. The guests are entertained by poets, musicians, dancers and a philosopher, but the principal purpose of the gathering is to drink and make conversation.

more wine!
A slave struggles with an amphora (large jar) of wine. The Greeks' favourite drink is normally drunk young, mixed with water. The best wine is said to come from the island of Chios.

slave and guard dog

well

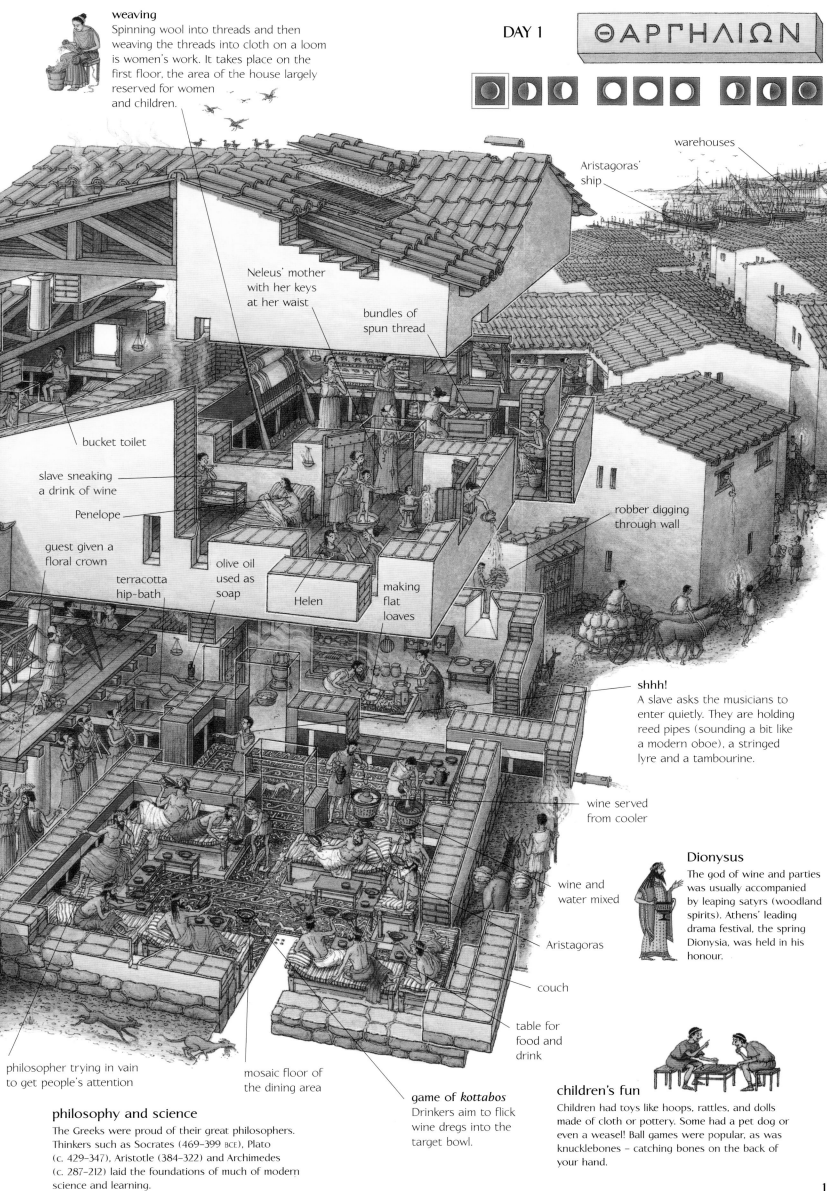

weaving
Spinning wool into threads and then weaving the threads into cloth on a loom is women's work. It takes place on the first floor, the area of the house largely reserved for women and children.

warehouses

Aristagoras' ship

Neleus' mother with her keys at her waist

bundles of spun thread

bucket toilet

slave sneaking a drink of wine

Penelope

robber digging through wall

guest given a floral crown

terracotta hip-bath

olive oil used as soap

Helen

making flat loaves

shhh!
A slave asks the musicians to enter quietly. They are holding reed pipes (sounding a bit like a modern oboe), a stringed lyre and a tambourine.

wine served from cooler

Dionysus
The god of wine and parties was usually accompanied by leaping satyrs (woodland spirits). Athens' leading drama festival, the spring Dionysia, was held in his honour.

wine and water mixed

Aristagoras

couch

table for food and drink

philosopher trying in vain to get people's attention

mosaic floor of the dining area

game of *kottabos*
Drinkers aim to flick wine dregs into the target bowl.

children's fun
Children had toys like hoops, rattles, and dolls made of cloth or pottery. Some had a pet dog or even a weasel! Ball games were popular, as was knucklebones – catching bones on the back of your hand.

philosophy and science
The Greeks were proud of their great philosophers. Thinkers such as Socrates (469–399 BCE), Plato (c. 429–347), Aristotle (384–322) and Archimedes (c. 287–212) laid the foundations of much of modern science and learning.

11

Entering the harbour at Delos

After saying goodbye to mum and our sisters, we left in one of dad's cargo boats. We sailed by day, moving from island to island. On the second morning we hit a storm and I was horribly seasick. Peri just laughed. Later, entering Delos harbour, we passed an amazing sacred Athenian warship. Peri and I waved, but dad only muttered grumpily that it had probably been paid for by tribute collected from hard-up Milesians.

Poseidon

The trident-wielding Poseidon, one of Zeus' brothers, ruled the kingdom of the seas. The Athenians held him in great respect because of their seafaring traditions and because he may have been father of their local hero Theseus.

slave transport ship

ship's sponsor

captain at the helm

leather curtain

mast

hoplite

priest

rowing master

yard and sail

seafaring

Ships and the sea, important to most Greeks, were vital to Athenians. Their wealth came mostly from overseas trade and tribute, and their powerful navy was a mighty weapon for attack and defence.

fishing

The Greeks ate vast quantities of fish and even imported extra supplies from the Black Sea. Fish was eaten fresh or preserved by salting or drying.

octopus   squid   tuna   mackerel

owl

A shield decorated with an owl is associated with the wise, 'owl-eyed' goddess Athene after whom Athens is named.

shipwright making repairs

edge-to-edge planks

bailing

oak keel

Ares

Ares, the bloody, merciless yet sometimes cowardly god of war, was hated by his parents, Zeus and Hera. He had only one admirer, Hades, ruler of the Underworld, as Ares' antics helped populate his kingdom of dead souls.

Scythian archer

thick rope to keep hull from sagging

rowers
Athenian men work the triremes (warships) as part of their military service. A trireme is powered by 170 oarsmen, 85 on each side in three tiers. The shape of the oars is different on each tier.

greased leather cushion

trireme
This special kind of ship is built of lighter wood on a heavy oak keel. The simple design allows Athens to build up to 200 ships a year.

eye motif

Delos
The sacred island of Delos gave its name to a league dedicated to resisting the Persians. The league – and Delos – soon came under strong Athenian control. In 426 BCE Athens ordered that no one was to die or be born on the island.

storm damage

temple

Delos town

Peri

Neleus

paidagogos

Aristagoras

steering oar

captain

pricey wood
Timber is scarce in southern Greece, making a wooden trireme a highly expensive piece of military equipment. Only Athens, with its rich silver mines and plentiful tribute, can afford to buy enough wood to build a large fleet.

settlements and colonies
The defeat of the Persians left Athens controlling a network of city-states around the Aegean Sea. Greeks also settled further afield, from Massilia in what is now southern France to Tell Sukas in Syria.

sea spear
36 metres long, 5.5 metres wide and capable of a maximum speed of about 18 kilometres an hour, a trireme was designed to skim over the water and pierce an enemy ship below the waterline with its deadly ram.

lead sheeting on hull

bronze ram

The silver mines at Laurion

At Thorikos we stayed with one of dad's business friends. Dad explained that he was going to Athens because his agent there, Lyrias, had been stealing his money. Our host reckoned the Athenians had enough money without taking dad's. He showed us what he meant by giving us a tour of Athens' huge silver mine at Laurion. When Peri started messing about and fell into a tank, it was my turn to laugh!

slag heap

Hera
After being rescued from the tank, Peri gave thanks to Hera. The sister-wife of Zeus and queen of the gods, Hera was the guardian of women, the home and children. She could be cruel, though, particularly towards her husband's girlfriends.

sorting ore

ventilation shaft

fire to create ventilation draft

pounding ore into chippings

oil lamp
Oil lamps burn olive oil, one of the many uses the Greeks make of the precious olive tree that was Athene's gift to Athens.

milling chippings into powder

dead slave

ladder

slavery
In Greece, as in all ancient societies, slavery was regarded as normal. Slaves were seen as objects, not people, and their owners could do more or less what they wanted with them.

rock pillar

ore removed from workface

mine slave
Appalling working conditions mean that mine slaves (usually prisoners of war) rarely survive more than a year or two. Consequently, they have to be carefully guarded in case they try to rebel or escape.

seam of silver ore 80 metres below ground

children breaking up ore

ΘΑΡΓΗΛΙΩΝ

arid landscape
Over thousands of years grazing animals and human woodcutters have gradually removed the covering vegetation, leaving the landscape of southern Greece arid and barren.

rainwater collected for silver processing

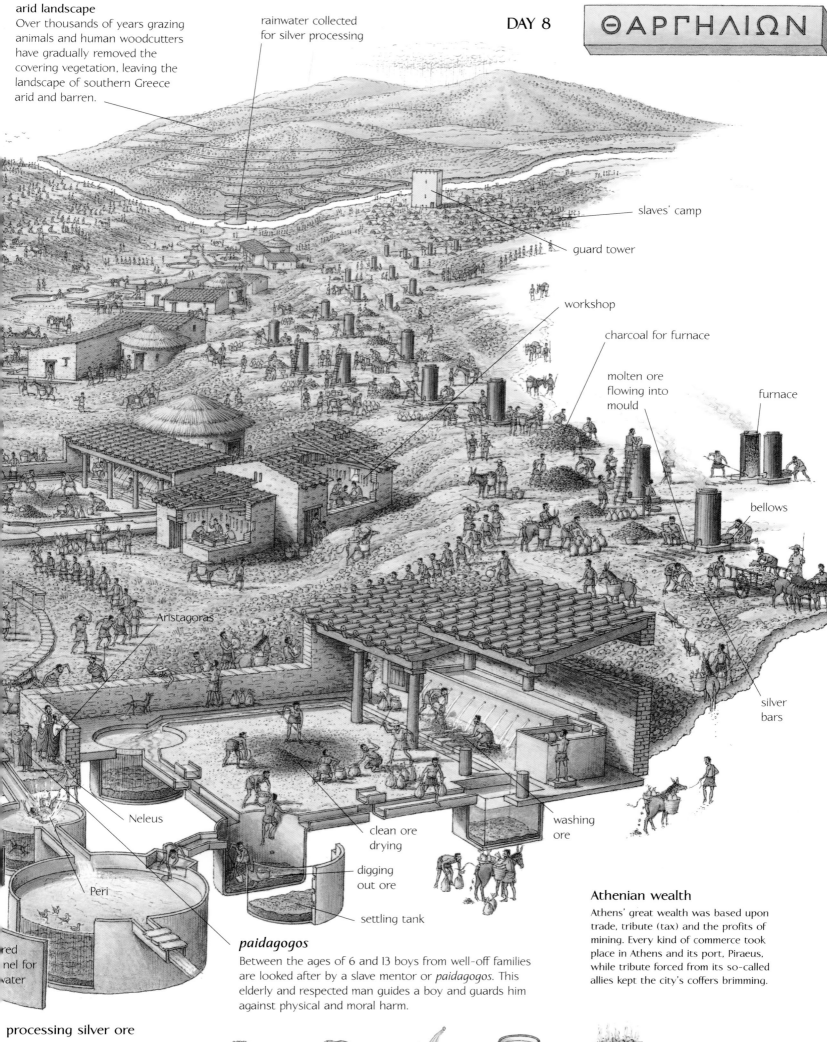

slaves' camp

guard tower

workshop

charcoal for furnace

molten ore flowing into mould

furnace

bellows

silver bars

Aristagoras

Neleus

Peri

washing ore

clean ore drying

digging out ore

settling tank

red nel for water

paidagogos
Between the ages of 6 and 13 boys from well-off families are looked after by a slave mentor or *paidagogos*. This elderly and respected man guides a boy and guards him against physical and moral harm.

Athenian wealth
Athens' great wealth was based upon trade, tribute (tax) and the profits of mining. Every kind of commerce took place in Athens and its port, Piraeus, while tribute forced from its so-called allies kept the city's coffers brimming.

processing silver ore

| ore is mined underground | ore is sorted by weight and colour to remove limestone | metallic ore is pounded into chippings | chippings are ground to dust | washing separates dirt from heavier metal-bearing ore | ore collects in settling tanks | clean ore is melted in a charcoal furnace | liquid silver solidifies in bars |

15

Piraeus, the port of Athens

We finally reached Piraeus, the port of the city of Athens. I'd never dreamed of so many ships and so much cargo! That morning Peri had said he wanted to be a wrestler, like Boulos, and I'd said he was far too clumsy. My point was proved when, as dad was changing money, Peri knocked over a jar of really expensive wine. The owner made dad pay, which turned him even more anti-Athens.

naval dockyard
Athens' triremes would quickly become waterlogged if they remained at sea for long. Consequently, a huge naval dockyard is needed to store and repair them.

sail loft

arsenal for storing trireme equipment

warehouse

ox cart

rainwater spout

banking table

official set of weights and measures

Neleus

Peri in trouble

iron ingots

almonds

bales of cloth

rope

shields

Aristagoras

millstones

raisins

metic businessman
Metics are Greeks who have come to live in Athens and do business there. Their skill and hard work have helped to build the city's prosperity, although they have no say in the government and cannot own property.

coinage
Coins were invented in Lydia (in present-day Turkey) and adopted by the Greeks in the 6th century BCE. Athens' owl-stamped coins, handmade from the silver of Laurion, were of the highest quality.

imports

As the territory around Athens (Attica) did not provide sufficient produce to feed the city, tonnes of grain were imported each year. There was also a ready market for luxuries like ivory, gold, silver, silk and perfumes.

exports

Goods made in Athens were in demand right across the Mediterranean. Most popular were earthenware jars (amphoras) of wine, fine pottery, and a variety of items fashioned from iron or bronze.

citizenship

Citizens were those born into families that had lived in and around Athens since the city's foundation. All male citizens took part in government and had to do military service. Women and children had few rights and were under the protection of their male relatives.

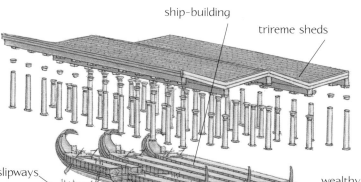

ship-building

trireme sheds

Demeter

The mystical goddess of corn and all fruits of the earth, Demeter was also closely linked to the Underworld: her daughter Persephone was married to the grim lord Hades.

slipways

wealthy Athenian citizen sponsoring a warship

harbour wall

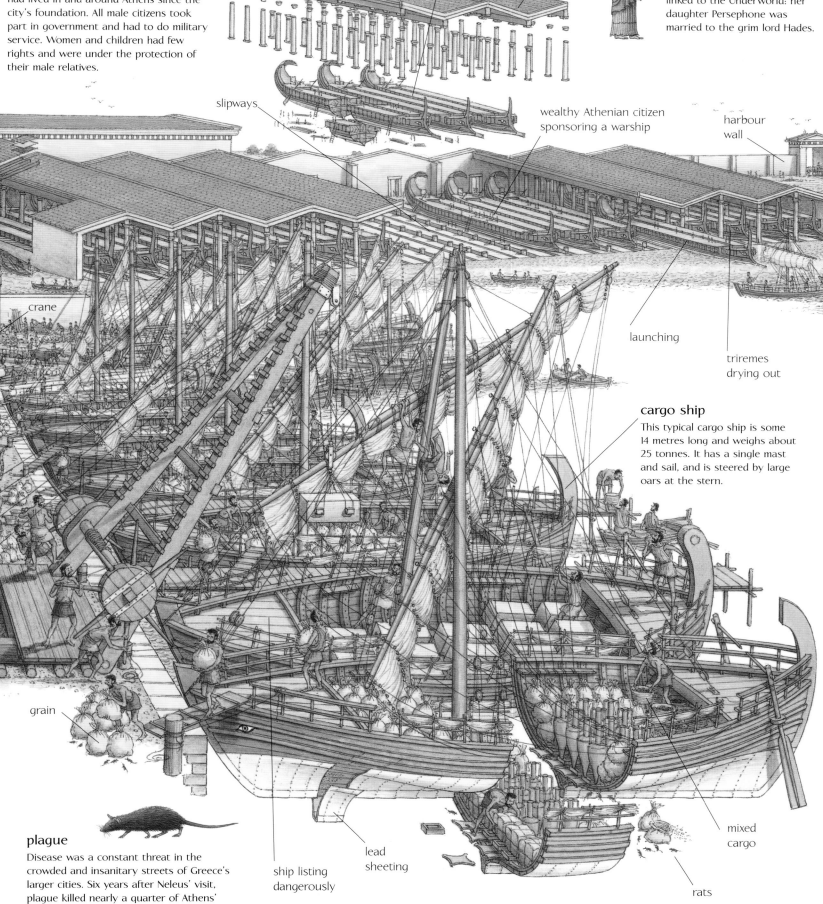

crane

launching

triremes drying out

cargo ship

This typical cargo ship is some 14 metres long and weighs about 25 tonnes. It has a single mast and sail, and is steered by large oars at the stern.

grain

mixed cargo

plague

Disease was a constant threat in the crowded and insanitary streets of Greece's larger cities. Six years after Neleus' visit, plague killed nearly a quarter of Athens' population. It was probably brought to the city by rats coming ashore at Piraeus.

ship listing dangerously

lead sheeting

rats

17

ΘΑΡΓΗΛΙΩΝ

Through Athens' crowded streets

I was disappointed with Athens. The greatest city in the world had majestic buildings and noble-looking people, of course, but there was too much foul-smelling dirt for my liking – and too many shady characters lurking in dark corners. To save money we stayed at a friend's house. Dad met with Aspasia and some experts on the law, and they worked together on his case. If he didn't win, our visit to Olympia would be cancelled.

Theseus
Theseus was Athens' favourite hero. The most famous of his many adventures was slaying the Minotaur, a bull-headed monster that lived at the heart of a labyrinth (maze) on the island of Crete.

Aspasia
Miletus-born Aspasia was the girlfriend of Pericles, one of Athens' greatest leaders. She lived in Athens from about 440 BCE. Unlike most Greek women, she was well educated and able to match the intellectual skills of men.

teacher
All schools are private and fee-paying. This schoolmaster is holding a class in the house where he lives. He teaches reading, writing and mathematics.

workers making small pottery figures

furniture shop

products for market

carpenter's workshop

sculptor

ironworks

cobbler's workshop

fuller's workshop for washing cloth

buildings of the Agora

paidagogos

jeweller's workshop

charcoal store

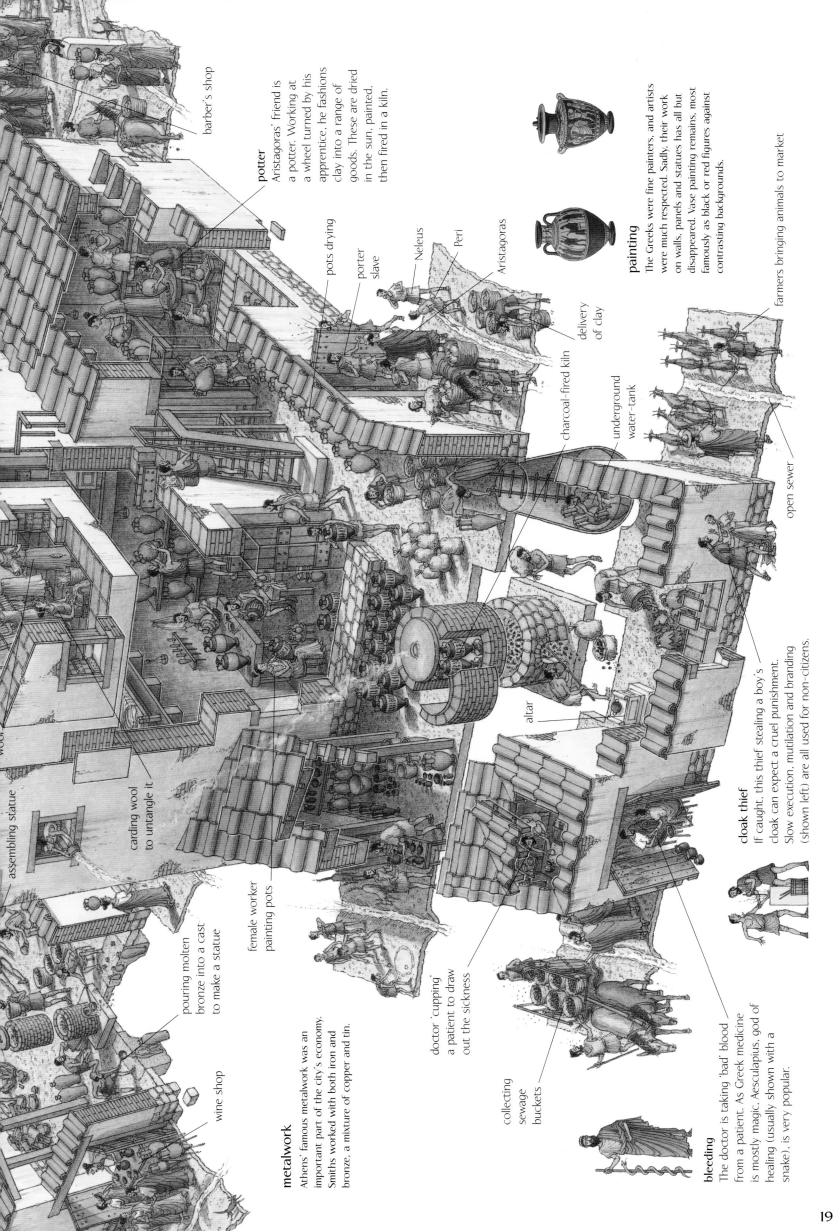

barber's shop

potter
Aristagoras' friend is a potter. Working at a wheel turned by his apprentice, he fashions clay into a range of goods. These are dried in the sun, painted, then fired in a kiln.

pots drying

porter slave

Neleus

Peri

Aristagoras

painting
The Greeks were fine painters, and artists were much respected. Sadly, their work on walls, panels and statues has all but disappeared. Vase painting remains, most famously as black or red figures against contrasting backgrounds.

delivery of clay

farmers bringing animals to market

charcoal-fired kiln

underground water-tank

open sewer

altar

metalwork
Athens' famous metalwork was an important part of the city's economy. Smiths worked with both iron and bronze, a mixture of copper and tin.

assembling statue

carding wool to untangle it

pouring molten bronze into a cast to make a statue

wine shop

female worker painting pots

doctor 'cupping' a patient to draw out the sickness

collecting sewage buckets

cloak thief
If caught, this thief stealing a boy's cloak can expect a cruel punishment. Slow execution, mutilation and branding (shown left) are all used for non-citizens.

bleeding
The doctor is taking 'bad' blood from a patient. As Greek medicine is mostly magic, Aesculapius, god of healing (usually shown with a snake), is very popular.

19

Shopping in the Agora

We explored the Agora while dad finally had his day in court. As I examined a figurine that I wanted to buy for mum, a cutpurse stole my money. Luckily, our *paidagogos* grabbed him and sent Peri off to fetch the Scythian police. At that moment dad turned up, waving his arms and grinning like Jason when he grabbed the Golden Fleece. He'd won! Lyrias was guilty and had to repay all the money. Our trip to Olympia was on!

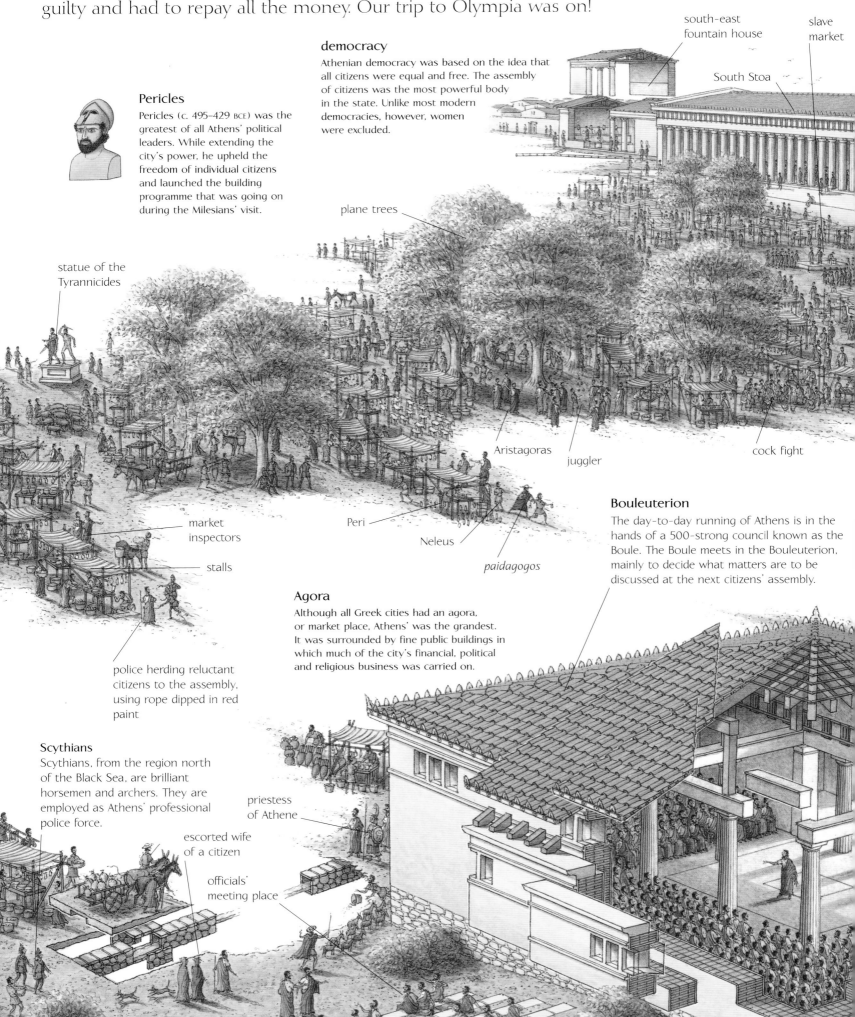

Pericles

Pericles (c. 495–429 BCE) was the greatest of all Athens' political leaders. While extending the city's power, he upheld the freedom of individual citizens and launched the building programme that was going on during the Milesians' visit.

democracy

Athenian democracy was based on the idea that all citizens were equal and free. The assembly of citizens was the most powerful body in the state. Unlike most modern democracies, however, women were excluded.

south-east fountain house

slave market

South Stoa

plane trees

statue of the Tyrannicides

Aristagoras

juggler

cock fight

market inspectors

Peri

Neleus

paidagogos

stalls

Bouleuterion

The day-to-day running of Athens is in the hands of a 500-strong council known as the Boule. The Boule meets in the Bouleuterion, mainly to decide what matters are to be discussed at the next citizens' assembly.

Agora

Although all Greek cities had an agora, or market place, Athens' was the grandest. It was surrounded by fine public buildings in which much of the city's financial, political and religious business was carried on.

police herding reluctant citizens to the assembly, using rope dipped in red paint

Scythians

Scythians, from the region north of the Black Sea, are brilliant horsemen and archers. They are employed as Athens' professional police force.

priestess of Athene

escorted wife of a citizen

officials' meeting place

ephaestus

nly in Athens was there a mple of the fire god Hephaestus. upposedly lame, this ingenious n of Zeus and Hera was not opular elsewhere. The Athenians ed him because he watched er their many smiths.

Aphrodite

According to legend, Aphrodite, the elegant goddess of beauty and love, was born out of sea foam. She became the wife of Hephaestus and the lover of Ares.

Athenian law

When a citizen was charged with breaking Athens' carefully worded law, the case was argued before a jury of several hundred citizens. They reached their decision by a secret vote, using a hollow voting token to indicate a guilty verdict, a solid one if they felt the accused was innocent.

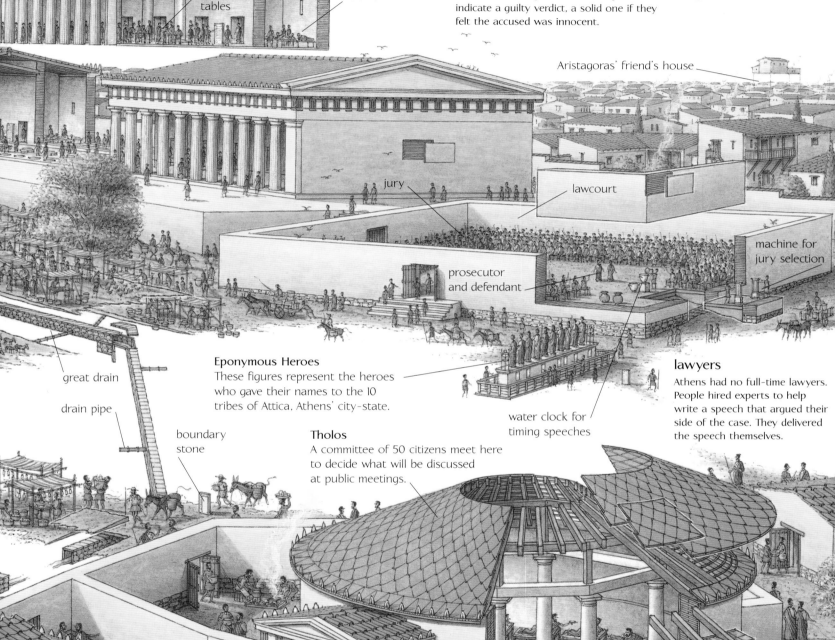

mud-brick walls

banking tables

dining rooms

Aristagoras' friend's house

jury

lawcourt

machine for jury selection

prosecutor and defendant

great drain

drain pipe

Eponymous Heroes

These figures represent the heroes who gave their names to the 10 tribes of Attica, Athens' city-state.

lawyers

Athens had no full-time lawyers. People hired experts to help write a speech that argued their side of the case. They delivered the speech themselves.

water clock for timing speeches

boundary stone

Tholos

A committee of 50 citizens meet here to decide what will be discussed at public meetings.

official weights and measures

market inspectors checking a roof tile

army officers

ostracism

Once a year, Athenian citizens could vote to ostracize (send out of the country) one of their number for 10 years. Ostracism, not necessarily a disgrace, was a means of getting rid of powerful men who might threaten democracy. Votes were written on pieces of broken pottery (ostraka).

21

The Acropolis and theatre of Dionysus

Dad's opinion of Athens had changed completely. He now loved the city and wanted to live there. Horrified, I begged him to check first with the oracle at Delphi. He agreed. Before we left, we climbed the Acropolis, gave thanks to Athene, and visited the theatre. Here the famous poet Sophocles was rehearsing his play *Ajax*. Guess who ruined the show? Wandering backstage in an actor's mask, Peri tripped and crashed noisily down some wooden steps.

frize carved with festival scenes

Ionic-style column

chest of coins

bronze statue of Athene, 9 metres tall

Jason
The legendary hero Jason sailed in the *Argo*, crewed by the Argonauts, to fetch the Golden Fleece. After many adventures, with the help of the witch Medea he stole the fleece from its guardian dragon. His story was often dramatized.

Acropolis
Like many Greek cities, Athens is based around a rocky fortress or 'acropolis'. Originally for defence, by the time of Neleus and Peri the Athenian Acropolis has also become a sacred site.

treasury
Here, in the largest of the city's treasure stores, much of its wealth is stored. A good deal of it is in the form of silver gathered from the mines at Laurion.

winch

new stone seats

wagons bringing stone

old wooden seating

buttres

stone seats for dignitaries

theatre Dionysus

chorus

Ajax

capstan

mason with mallet and chisel

tragedy
Greek tragedies usually told mythological stories in which disaster struck a famous person. Much of the action took place off stage. The highly emotional plays generally ended in violence and death.

comedy
Greek comedies, performed by male actors wearing masks and indecent costumes, made fun of gods and leading figures of the day.

wooden backdrop

table for masks

Peri

marble roof tiles

central aisle

Athene
The many-talented goddess Athene sprang fully armed from the head of Zeus. Essentially a war goddess, she became Attica's special deity when its citizens chose her gift of the olive over Poseidon's gift of a horse.

gold and ivory statue of Athene

pool to reflect light

carvings

decoration on the highest point

vertical decoration (triglyph)

finished sculpture being winched into position

painting a sculpture

deep foundations of limestone

Parthenon
The magnificent marble temple of Athene, built in the Doric style and decorated with sculptures by Pheidias, is nearly finished. Pericles has conceived it as a gleaming symbol of Athens' power and glory.

Odeon
Pericles' Odeon is a huge covered hall for musical events and drama rehearsal. Its pyramid-shaped roof, supposedly based on the design of tent of the defeated Persian king Xerxes, is supported by 90 columns.

recycled masts of Persian ships captured at Salamis

Aristagoras and Neleus

Sophocles
The popular dramatist Sophocles tries out his new tragedy *Ajax* for possible performance in next year's drama festival.

Orpheus
The legendary lyre-player Orpheus, one of the Argonauts, was Greece's sublime musician. His music charmed all people and objects. His life ended tragically after he failed to bring his wife Eurydice back from the Underworld.

musical contest

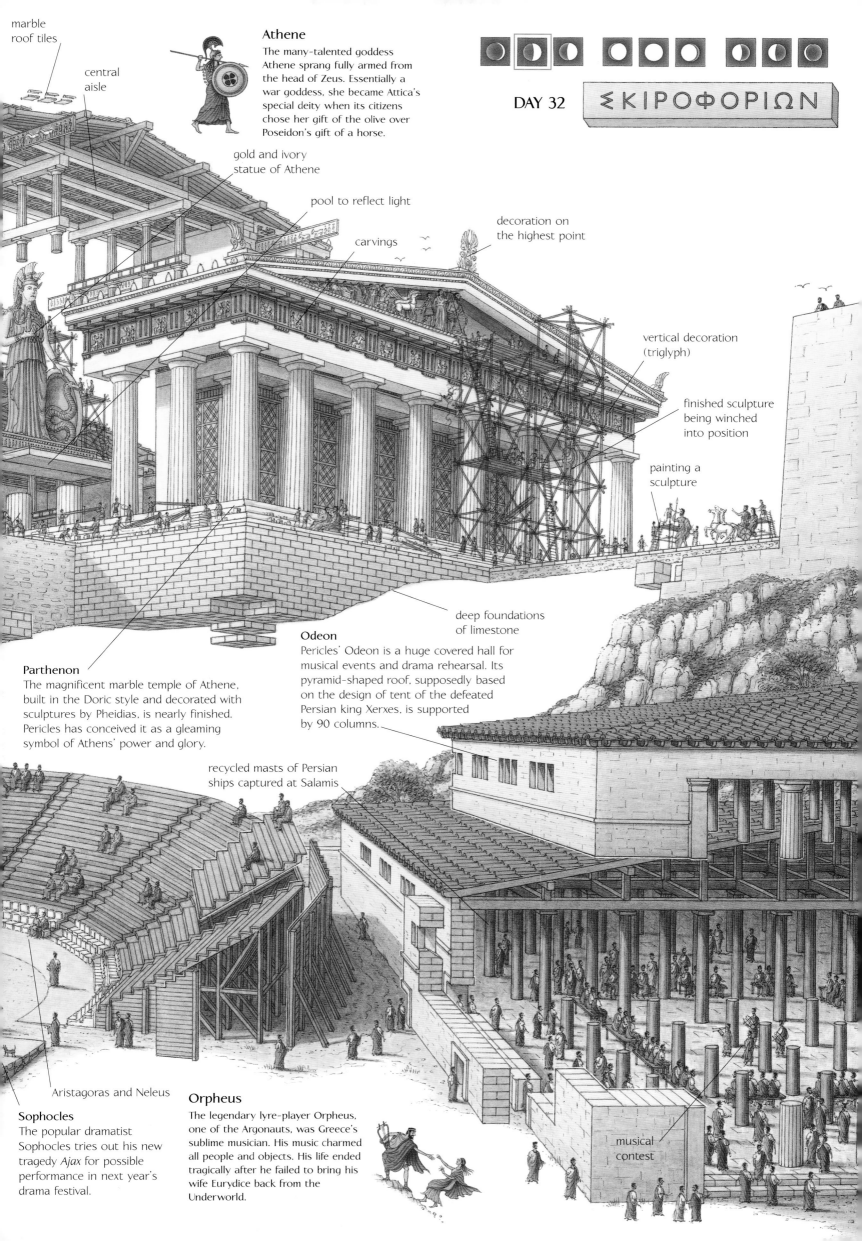

Apollo's temple at Delphi

We sailed to Delphi past the site of the Greeks' great naval victory at Salamis. The shrine of Apollo, the navel of the Earth, is an eerie place. Should we stay at Miletus, we asked the god, or move to Athens? I was shaking with fear when the priest brought the answer: 'Wisdom will appear at Olympia.' Dad said this meant if Boulos became Olympic wrestling champion, we'd stay in Miletus. If not, we'd move.

river god

Leto, a female Titan, mother of Apollo

deities

Doric-style capital

gold-plated doors

waiting chamber

Apollo

the snake-monster Python

Gaia (Earth), mother of the Python

deities

sphinx

river god

Apollo

eagle

sanctuary of Apollo

The sanctuary, close to where the god once performed heroic deeds, lay at the heart of one of Greece's most popular places of pilgrimage.

oracles

The commonest way for men and gods to communicate was through an oracle. This was a shrine where a priest or priestess could contact the resident deity, usually to obtain an (ambiguous) answer to a question.

dedications

Delphi's many statues, armour and other offerings were dedicated to Apollo in thanks for his assistance. This famous statue of a charioteer was a mark of gratitude for a chariot team's victory in the local games.

Apollo

The beautiful young god Apollo, a perfect Greek male, was associated with reason, music, archery, medicine and, above all, prophesy. The island of Delos, where he and his sister Artemis were born, was sacred to him.

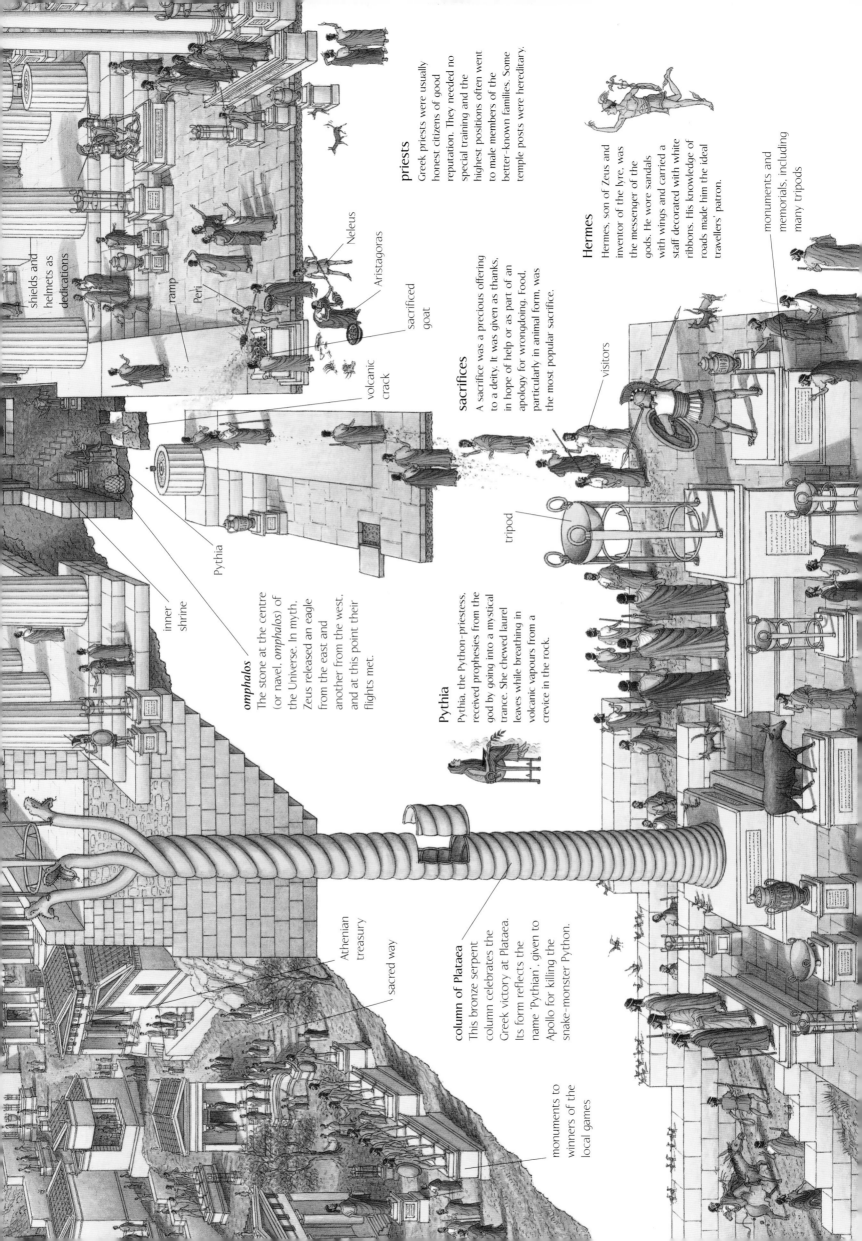

shields and helmets as dedications

ramp

Peri

Neleus

Aristagoras

sacrificed goat

volcanic crack

Pythia

inner shrine

omphalos
The stone at the centre (or navel, *omphalos*) of the Universe. In myth, Zeus released an eagle from the east and another from the west, and at this point their flights met.

Pythia
Pythia, the Python-priestess, received prophesies from the god by going into a mystical trance. She chewed laurel leaves while breathing in volcanic vapours from a crevice in the rock.

Athenian treasury

sacred way

column of Plataea
This bronze serpent column celebrates the Greek victory at Plataea. Its form reflects the name 'Pythian', given to Apollo for killing the snake-monster Python.

monuments to winners of the local games

priests
Greek priests were usually honest citizens of good reputation. They needed no special training and the highest positions often went to male members of the better-known families. Some temple posts were hereditary.

sacrifices
A sacrifice was a precious offering to a deity. It was given as thanks, in hope of help or as part of an apology for wrongdoing. Food, particularly in animal form, was the most popular sacrifice.

Hermes
Hermes, son of Zeus and inventor of the lyre, was the messenger of the gods. He wore sandals with wings and carried a staff decorated with white ribbons. His knowledge of roads made him the ideal travellers' patron.

visitors

tripod

monuments and memorials, including many tripods

The Olympic Games

Boulos' wrestling final was on the third day of the Games. His opponent was an Athenian, and a huge crowd gathered to watch. Peri and I climbed a tree to get a good view. Imagine our joy when, after a long fight, Boulos triumphed. We were staying in Miletus! Peri was so happy he fell out of the tree. He'll never be an athlete, just as I'll never be an Athenian.

Olympic Games

After completing one of his legendary labours, Greece's most famous hero Heracles founded the Olympic Games in honour of his father Zeus. Staged every fourth summer from 776 BCE, they were open to all males from across the Greek world.

Olympic Truce

The Olympic Truce was a one-month period (later three months) during which warfare and legal disputes between states were banned. This meant the Games were not disrupted by fighting, and competitors and visitors could attend in safety.

Zeus

The position of Zeus as king of the gods was based upon sheer power. He became king by killing his Titan father, Kronos. He was father of five other deities as well as many other children by different mothers.

the Altis

This walled part of the site, originally an olive grove, is sacred to Zeus. It contains the temples of Zeus and Hera, treasuries, and other religious structures.

wrestling

This type of wrestling is won by throwing an opponent to the ground three times. In the more violent 'pankration' kicking, punching and strangling are allowed, but not biting or gouging.

hill of Kronos

Hera and Hermes

temple of Hera

paintings of women athletes

Boulos

judge

Neleus

Aristagoras

Peri

workshop of the sculptor Pheidias

winch

Pheidias

ivory-plated panel

gold and ivory statue of Zeus being built to replace the old image in the temple

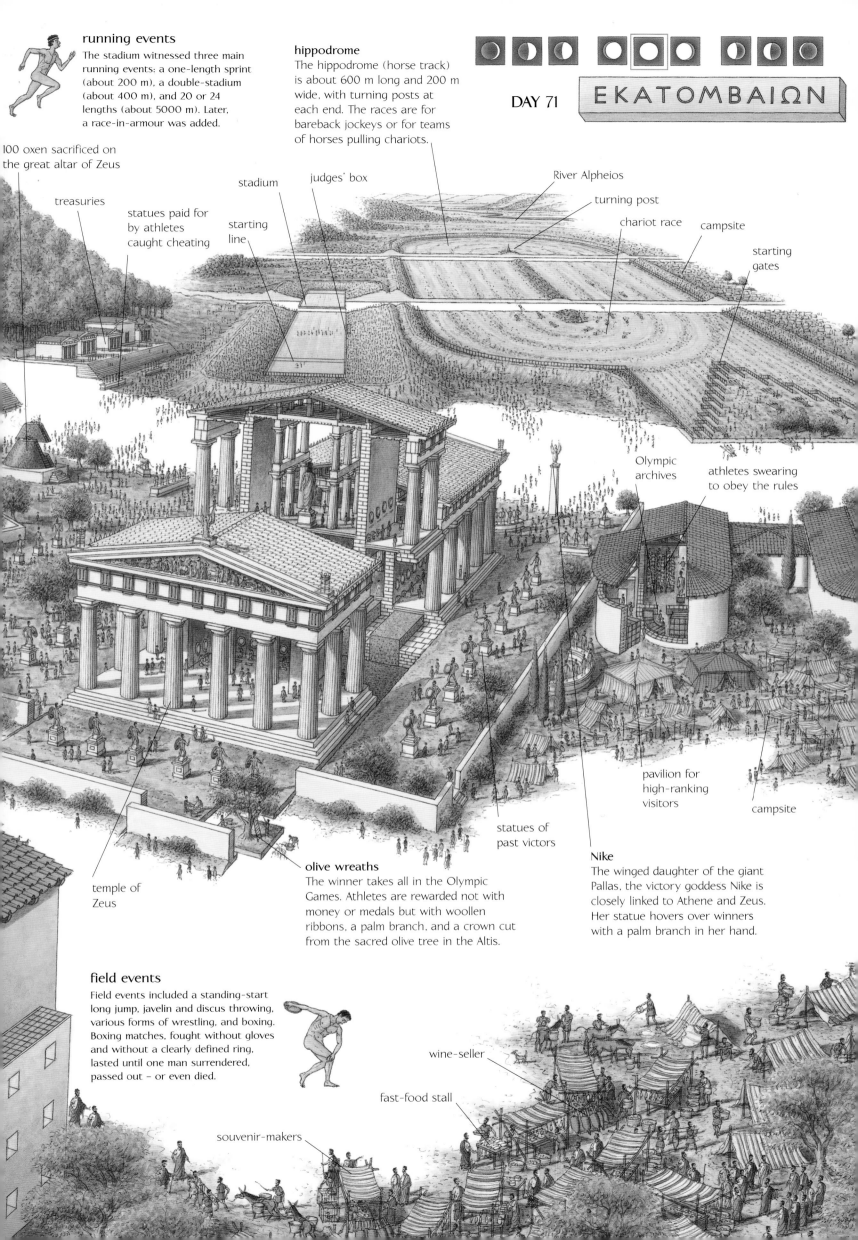

running events
The stadium witnessed three main running events: a one-length sprint (about 200 m), a double-stadium (about 400 m), and 20 or 24 lengths (about 5000 m). Later, a race-in-armour was added.

hippodrome
The hippodrome (horse track) is about 600 m long and 200 m wide, with turning posts at each end. The races are for bareback jockeys or for teams of horses pulling chariots.

100 oxen sacrificed on the great altar of Zeus

treasuries

statues paid for by athletes caught cheating

stadium

starting line

judges' box

River Alpheios

turning post

chariot race

campsite

starting gates

Olympic archives

athletes swearing to obey the rules

temple of Zeus

statues of past victors

pavilion for high-ranking visitors

campsite

olive wreaths
The winner takes all in the Olympic Games. Athletes are rewarded not with money or medals but with woollen ribbons, a palm branch, and a crown cut from the sacred olive tree in the Altis.

Nike
The winged daughter of the giant Pallas, the victory goddess Nike is closely linked to Athene and Zeus. Her statue hovers over winners with a palm branch in her hand.

field events
Field events included a standing-start long jump, javelin and discus throwing, various forms of wrestling, and boxing. Boxing matches, fought without gloves and without a clearly defined ring, lasted until one man surrendered, passed out – or even died.

wine-seller

fast-food stall

souvenir-makers

Glossary

acropolis: a fortified and often sacred high point at the heart of a Greek city.

agora: an open space in a city for markets, meetings, games and so forth.

amphora: a pottery wine jar with handles.

Attica: the name of the city-state of which Athens was the capital.

branding: deliberately marking the skin with a red-hot iron.

bronze: a tough mixture of tin and copper.

democracy: government by the citizens.

Doric: a simple and solid style of architecture.

frieze: a decorated stone band above the columns of a building.

Hades: see Underworld.

Homer: a semi-legendary poet who supposedly wrote the epic poems the *Iliad* (about the fall of Troy) and the *Odyssey* (about the travels of the hero Odysseus).

hoplite: a heavily armoured foot soldier equipped with a shield, sword and spear.

Ionia: a region that extends along the west coast of modern-day Turkey.

Ionic: a style of architecture featuring scroll-like decoration at the top of columns.

lyre: a musical instrument like a hand-held harp.

metic: a resident foreigner.

oracle: a place where people consulted a deity who was supposed to foretell the future.

paidagogos: a slave appointed to supervise children.

patron: a protector and helper.

philosopher: a 'lover of wisdom' and seeker after truth in all things.

sacrifice: an offering made to please a deity, usually involving killing and burning a valuable animal such as a goat or an ox.

shrine: a holy place for the worship and honouring of a deity.

sphinx: a mythical animal, usually shown with the body of a lion and a human head.

stoa: an open building, with a roof supported by columns, used for meetings.

symposium: an all-male drinking party.

Titans: the mythical first creatures on the Earth, who were defeated and replaced by the gods.

treasury: a place where money and valuable objects were stored, for future use or as gifts to a deity.

tribute: money or valuables paid by a weaker state to a more powerful one. Although in theory semi-voluntary, it was really a type of tax.

trident: a large three-pronged fork for fishing or fighting.

tripod: a three-footed support for vessels.

trireme: a warship with three banks of oars.

Underworld: also known as Hades, a region deep beneath the Earth where the dead went. It was ruled by a god who was also called Hades.

The Olympians

These were the 12 deities, known collectively as the Pantheon, believed to live on top of Mount Olympus.

Aphrodite

One legend says that Aphrodite, the elegant goddess of beauty and love, was born out of sea foam. Other sources say she was a child of Zeus. She became wife of Hephaestus, lover of Ares, and mother of Eros.

Apollo

The beautiful young god Apollo, a perfect Greek male, was associated with reason, music, archery, medicine, and above all prophesy, especially at the Delphic oracle. The island of Delos, where he and his twin sister Artemis were born, was sacred to him.

Ares

Ares, the bloody, merciless yet sometimes cowardly god of war, was hated by his parents, Zeus and Hera. He had only one admirer, Hades, ruler of the Underworld, because Ares' antics helped populate his kingdom of dead souls.

Artemis

The virgin deity Artemis was the goddess of hunting, animals and childbirth. She was also associated with the Moon. Her temple at Ephesus was one of the Seven Wonders of the ancient world.

Athene

Many-talented Athene, goddess of war and patron of arts and crafts, was wisdom in god-like form. She became Attica's special deity because when she offered its people the olive, they chose it over Poseidon's gift of a horse.

Demeter

The mystical goddess of corn and all fruits of the Earth, Demeter was also closely linked to the Underworld: her daughter Persephone was married to the grim lord Hades. Rituals in honour of Demeter focused on death and rebirth.

Dionysus

The god of wine and wild parties was usually accompanied by leaping satyrs (woodland spirits). Athens' leading drama festival, the spring Dionysia, was held in his honour. Some of the festivities associated with him were very wild and unrestrained.

Hephaestus

Hephaestus, son of Zeus and Hera, was the ingenious god of fire and metal-workers. His forge was under the volcanic Mount Etna. Athens, seeking protection for its many smiths, was the only city to honour him with a temple.

Hera

The sister-wife of Zeus and queen of the gods, Hera was the guardian of women, the home and children. She could be cruel, though, particularly towards her husband's innumerable girlfriends.

Hermes

Hermes, son of Zeus and inventor of the lyre, was the messenger of the gods. He wore sandals with wings and carried a staff decorated with white ribbons. His knowledge of roads made him the ideal travellers' patron.

Poseidon

The mighty Poseidon ruled the kingdom of the seas. He was one of Zeus' brothers and was usually shown carrying a trident. The Athenians held him in double respect because of their seafaring traditions and because he was supposedly the father of their local hero Theseus.

Zeus

Zeus was king of the gods. His authority was based upon sheer power – he became king, for example, by killing his Titan father, Kronos. Zeus was father of five Olympians and had many other children by different mothers. His name means 'sky'.

The Greek alphabet

The Greek alphabet, based on the Phoenician alphabet with the addition of vowels, appeared in the 8th century BCE. Our word 'alphabet' comes from its first two letters, alpha and beta. Here are the ancient Greek capital letters, with their names and English equivalents:

Α	alpha	a
Β	beta	b
Γ	gamma	g
Δ	delta	d
Ε	epsilon	short e
Ζ	zeta	z
Η	eta	long e
Θ	theta	th
Ι	iota	i
Κ	kappa	k
Λ	lambda	l
Μ	mu	m
Ν	nu	n
Ξ	xi	x
Ο	omicron	short o
Π	pi	p
Ρ	rho	r
Σ	sigma	s
Τ	tau	t
Υ	upsilon	u
Φ	phi	ph
Χ	chi	ch
Ψ	psi	psi
Ω	omega	long o

Index

OXFORD
UNIVERSITY PRESS

Great Clarendon Street, Oxford OX2 6DP

Oxford University Press is a department of the University of Oxford.
It furthers the University's objective of excellence in research, scholarship,
and education by publishing worldwide in

Oxford   New York

Auckland   Cape Town   Dar es Salaam   Hong Kong   Karachi
Kuala Lumpur   Madrid   Melbourne   Mexico City   Nairobi
New Delhi   Shanghai   Taipei   Toronto

With offices in

Argentina   Austria   Brazil   Chile   Czech Republic   France   Greece
Guatemala   Hungary   Italy   Japan   Poland   Portugal   Singapore
South Korea   Switzerland   Thailand   Turkey   Ukraine   Vietnam

Oxford is a registered trade mark of Oxford University Press
in the UK and in certain other countries

Illustrations © copyright Stephen Biesty 2006

Text © copyright Stewart Ross 2006

The moral rights of the author and illustrator have been asserted

Database right Oxford University Press (maker)

First published 2006

British Library Cataloguing in Publication Data

Data available

ISBN-13: 978-0-19-911176-3 (hardback)
ISBN-10: 0-19-911176-6 (hardback)

ISBN-13: 978-0-19-911511-2 (paperback)
ISBN-10: 0-19-911511-7 (paperback)

3 5 7 9 10 8 6 4 2

Printed in China